CODING UNPLUGGED

WITH ART

GETTING KID-CODERS OFF THE SCREEN AND ON THEIR FEET!

BY KAITLYN SIU
ILLUSTRATED BY DAVE SMITH

First published in Great Britain in 2023
by Wayland
Copyright © Hodder and Stoughton, 2023
All rights reserved

Commissioning Editor: Grace Glendinning
Project Manager: Em Stafford
Designer: Emma DeBanks
Illustrations: Dave Smith

HB ISBN: 978 1 5263 2192 3
PB ISBN: 978 1 5263 2193 0

Printed and bound in Dubai

Wayland, an imprint of
Hachette Children's Group
Part of Hodder and Stoughton
Carmelite House
50 Victoria Embankment
London EC4Y 0DZ

An Hachette UK Company
www.hachette.co.uk
www.hachettechildrens.co.uk

WARNING

We recommend adult supervision at all times while doing the activities in this book. Always be aware that craft materials may contain allergens, so check the packaging for allergens if there is a risk of an allergic reaction. Anyone with a known allergy must avoid these.

- Wear an apron and cover surfaces.
- Tie back long hair.
- Ask an adult for help with cutting.
- Check materials for allergens.

FSC
www.fsc.org

MIX
Paper from
responsible sources
FSC® C104740

CONTENTS

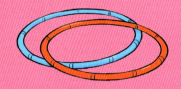

SCREEN-FREE CODING
WITH ART

Let's start a **CODING ADVENTURE** with art!
We're going to learn how to talk like computers
with fun art activities you can do at home.

The activities in this book are all **UNPLUGGED**,
which means you don't need a computer or
a screen to learn how to code. Most of them
involve getting together with friends and using
teamwork, taking it all outside if you like to get
lots of fresh air!

You'll be creating an origami dog one minute and spotting 'bugs' in a painting the next.

You won't believe where you can find coding at work – or how much fun coding with art can be!

GET YOUR PAINT POTS READY

AS THESE ACTIVITIES

ARE GOING TO REQUIRE SOME

CREATIVITY! ➤

WHAT IS CODING?

Coding is a process that helps people talk to computers in their own language. Computers aren't naturally clever like you! A computer doesn't understand what needs to be done unless the instructions are translated into 'COMPUTER CODE'.

If a computer is asked to draw a picture of the Sun, it wouldn't know how to do this automatically. A computer would need to be told how to do this in **VERY SPECIFIC STEPS**.

It would first need to know how to draw basic shapes and lines. Then it would need to be taught to draw a circle with lines around the edge to create the Sun.

By the end of this book, you're going to be talking in '**COMPUTER**' and will know how to give computers instructions that they will understand, with some fun art activities as inspiration!

REAL-LIFE ART MADE BY CODING

Did you know that coding is everywhere? Coding can even be seen in art we use every day. We wouldn't have **DIGITAL WALLPAPER, 3-D PRINTING** or **GRAPHICS** for video games without the magic of coding!

VIDEO GRAPHICS

DIGITAL WALLPAPER

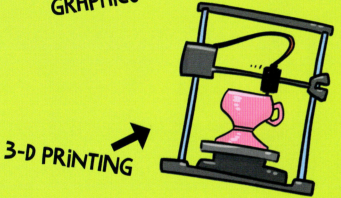

3-D PRINTING

KIDS CAN CODE TOO!

You don't need a lot of experience to learn how to code. In fact, there are **6 SIMPLE CODING IDEAS** you can learn that form the **FOUNDATION** of any coding program – and you can do it at any age.

CODING CONCEPTS

You may know some of these already, but you can turn the page to remind yourself, or use the next few pages as quick references when you start the art **ACTIVITIES** later in the book.

KEY CODING CONCEPT #1:
THE ALGORITHM

An **ALGORITHM** is an **INSTRUCTION** given to help complete a certain task.

An algorithm is a bit like a **RECIPE** for **BAKING** or a **KEY** on a **MAP**. If you don't know what all the symbols mean, you're not going to get very far!

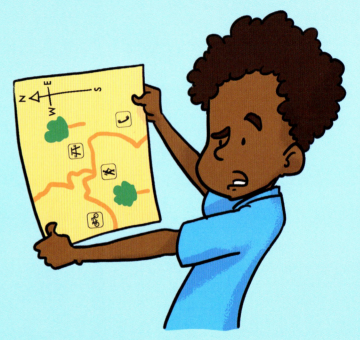

In art, we can use **KEYS** (algorithms) to complete 'paint by numbers' paintings. Each number represents a specific colour and, all together, the numbers create a beautiful work of art. If we don't follow all the instructions correctly our artwork might not come out clearly or it might show a different picture altogether!

KEY CODING CONCEPT #2:
SEQUENCE

SEQUENCE refers to the **ORDER** of steps
in your algorithm.

When you give **INSTRUCTIONS**, it's important to give them in the **CORRECT ORDER**. It wouldn't make sense to brush the canvas before putting paint on the brush. The order is important!

STEP 1
PUT ORANGE PAINT ON BRUSH.

STEP 2
SPREAD ORANGE PAINT ON TOP HALF OF CANVAS WITH BRUSH.

STEP 3
CLEAN BRUSH.

STEP 4
ALLOW TO DRY.

WHAT DO YOU THINK iS THE NEXT STEP?
(ANSWER ON PAGE 48)

If you're drawing a sunset, you'll want to build up your colours and time your drying steps carefully so you can show lots of details and your colours won't get too muddled!

KEY CODING CONCEPT #3:
LOOPS

A loop is a **SET** of **iNSTRUCTiONS** that repeat and repeat until a specific condition is met.

In coding we can draw a flower using a series of ovals that repeat in a specific pattern. The ovals make the shape of the petals and the drawing repeats until the flower is complete. Expert coders can draw really detailed scenes, all with code!

←OVALS

KEY CODING CONCEPT #4:
VARIABLES

A variable is a way of **HOLDING INFORMATION**.
It's like a box that keeps information inside it.

Variables can be **REPRESENTED** with **LETTERS, WORDS** or **NUMBERS**. In art, we can use variables to quickly change the impression of a picture. Imagine a picture of a beach with a beautiful blue sky.

We start by setting

SKY = BLUE

Now imagine the sky is a variable in our art. But what if we change the value of the sky variable? If we set the variable to be orange or grey, the feeling of our picture will completely change!

KEY CODING CONCEPT #5:
BRANCHING

Branching refers to making a **DECISION** based on what is **HAPPENING** or has **HAPPENED**.

If you don't have green paint, you might have to mix your own green from yellow and blue to do your painting. Or if you don't have green, you might decide to paint a tree in autumn. It's all about making a choice based on the condition.

IF NO **GREEN** PAINT?

THEN:

THEN:

Mix

USE

KEY CODING CONCEPT #6:
DECOMPOSITION

Decomposition refers to breaking something up into **SMALLER PARTS**.

This drawing of a skyline is actually made up of many different shapes and lines. Can you spot all the rectangles, squares and circles? Decomposition in art is about breaking down a big picture into smaller bits and pieces.

IT'S
ACTIVITY
TIME!
→

DECOMPOSITION AND ALGORITHMS UNPLUGGED: CODE WITH ORIGAMI

Origami is the art of **PAPER FOLDING**. These folded pieces are often made into small figures, animals, or other shapes that can be used as decorations.

I bet you didn't know that learning origami can also teach you how to code!

← ORIGAMI

In this activity, you and some friends can practise writing an 'origami-folding algorithm'. Once done, you'll also complete a decomposition challenge with your paper folds.

LET'S GET CODING!

MATERIALS YOU WILL NEED:

* ❋ Some square pieces of paper
* ❋ Two small tables
* ❋ Two chairs
* ❋ Origami folding instructions in this book

PAPER

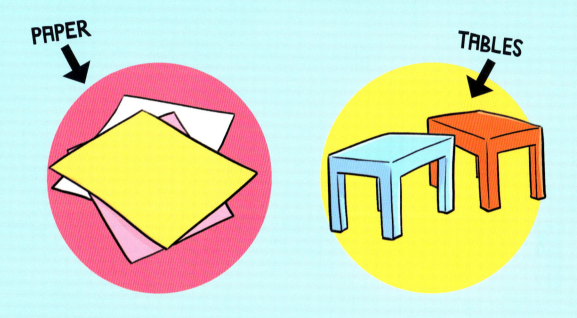

TABLES

CHAIRS

INSTRUCTIONS

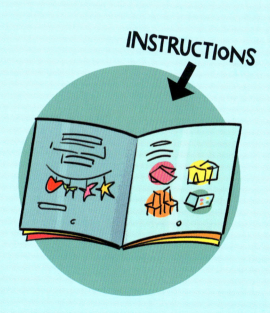

GAME
SET UP:

In this origami activity, you will be creating a simple folded dog face.

← SIMPLE FOLDED DOG FACE

The **KEY** to this algorithm activity is that only one origami coder will be able to see the illustrations in this book. That coder needs to explain the algorithm out loud to the other coder.

Together, you're learning just how **CHALLENGING** algorithms are for computers!

> DRAW A SUN! IT'S A YELLOW CIRCLE WITH YELLOW LINES ALL AROUND.

Remember, computers don't have eyes to see. They need to be given **VERY SPECIFIC** and **EXACT INSTRUCTIONS** with **LOTS OF DETAIL**. If computers aren't given the correct instructions, the outcome can be really silly!

BACK-TO-BACK

IMPORTANT!

DON'T TURN THIS PAGE UNTIL YOU'VE SET YOURSELF UP BACK-TO-BACK WITH A FRIEND AND DECIDED WHO'S GOING TO FOLLOW THE BOOK, AND WHO'S GOING TO FOLLOW THEIR FRIEND'S INSTRUCTIONS!

GAME PLAY!

ORIGAMI ALGORITHM

IF YOU'VE TURNED TO THIS PAGE YOU SHOULD BE SITTING **BACK-TO-BACK** WITH A FRIEND WHO **CANNOT SEE** THESE INSTRUCTIONS!

Each player gets a square piece of paper.

One coder uses the book, and one does as they're told by their friend!

Both coders need to fold the paper step-by-step. The coder using this book will need to explain in their own words the instructions to the other coder.

STEP 1

STEP 2

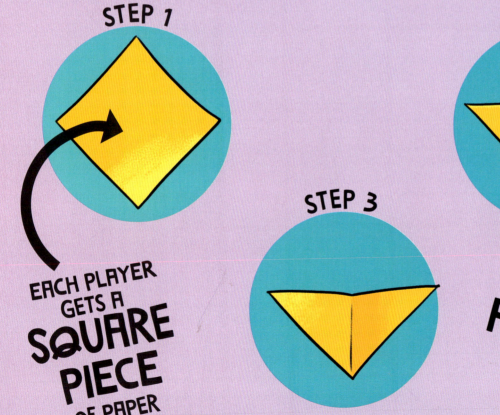

STEP 3

EACH PLAYER GETS A **SQUARE PIECE** OF PAPER

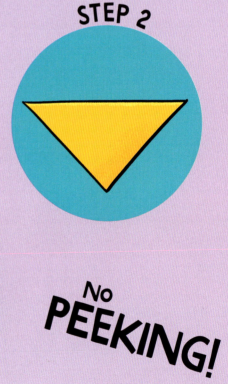

No **PEEKING!**

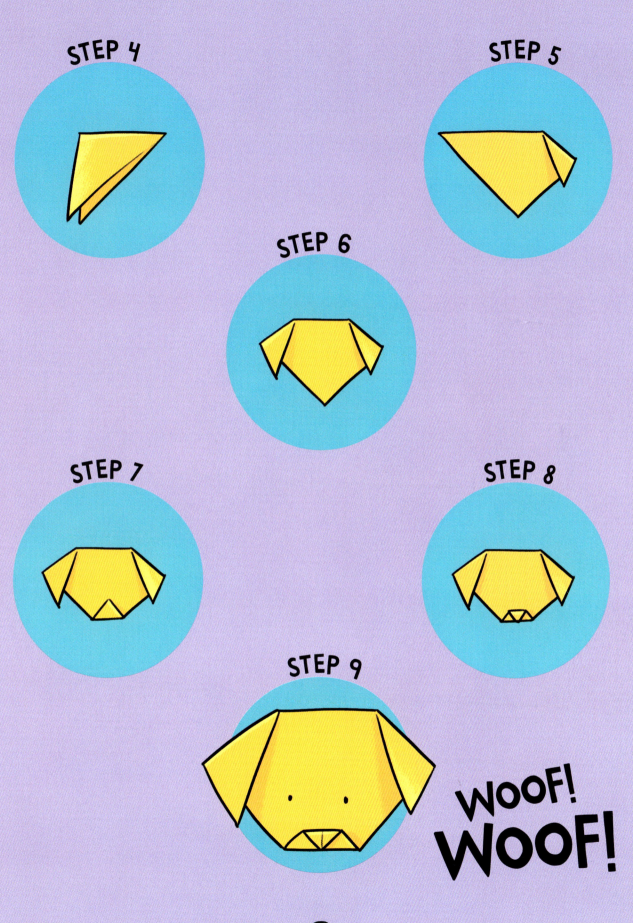

STEP 4

STEP 5

STEP 6

STEP 7

STEP 8

STEP 9

WOOF!
WOOF!

GAME PLAY: DEBUGGING

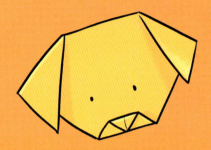

Once you've reached the final fold, face each other and check out your origami creations!

How well did the coder explain the steps? Did the second origami creation turn out right?

CHECK IT OUT!

If not, we will need to debug our algorithm.

**REMEMBER:
DEBUGGING
MEANS FIXING MISTAKES
IN THE CODE.**

Now both coders can look at the book and find out what went wrong, and where!

GAME PLAY: DECOMPOSITION CHALLENGE

Let's add an extra challenge and try **DECOMPOSING** origami as well. You may want lots of people on your Decomposers team for this one – it's definitely tricky!

Have one friend build an origami swan using the algorithm on the next page. They mustn't show the steps to the Decomposers.

IMPORTANT!

DO NOT TURN THIS PAGE UNTIL YOU DECIDE WHO IS THE BUILDER AND WHO WHO IS A DECOMPOSER!

21

REMEMBER:
DON'T
SHOW THESE STEPS
TO THE DECOMPOSERS.

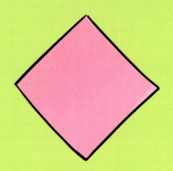

1 Start with your square paper rotated to form a diamond shape.

2 Fold the paper in half to make a triangle.

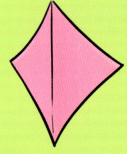

3 Unfold the paper.

4 Fold the right and left corner of the diamond base towards the centre crease line.

5 Flip over your folded paper.

6 Fold the left and right edges towards the centre crease.

7 Fold the bottom point to the top point.

8 Fold the top point down by about a finger width to create the swan's head.

9 Fold the right and left edges backwards along the centre crease.

10 Pull the swan's neck forward a bit.

11 Pull the swan's head up and crease it again if needed.

THE DECOMPOSERS

The folder gives the finished swan to the Decomposers.

As a team, try to come up with an origami algorithm by starting **BACKWARDS** from the finished product! Use a blank piece of paper to draw out your steps.

Compare your decomposed swan algorithm to the official instructions on the previous page. How did you do? Where do you need to debug?

FINISHED
SWAN

SPOT THE CODE!

Which coding concepts do you see at work here in this cat art lesson? It's amazing that coding concepts are found even in drawing pictures. Try your own drawing, and maybe make your own idea for an animal you can teach others to draw with a simple step-by-step process.

24

(ANSWER ON PAGE 48)

SEQUENCING UNPLUGGED: EGG CARTON CODING ACTIVITY

Let's have fun with some **PAINT** and a **SIMPLE EGG CARTON**. This egg carton craft will introduce you to coding in a creative way.

This unplugged coding activity will teach you to sequence an algorithm to capture all the egg prizes and avoid the hot lava rocks.

LET'S GET SEQUENCING!

MATERIALS YOU WILL NEED:

* Multiple large egg carton flats (or smaller egg cartons taped together)
* Red paint
* A small figurine to act as the 'robot'

* Decorated plastic eggs to act as prizes (filling them with treats is optional!)
* Stickers and paint pens or other materials for decorating the outside of your eggs

EGG CARTONS

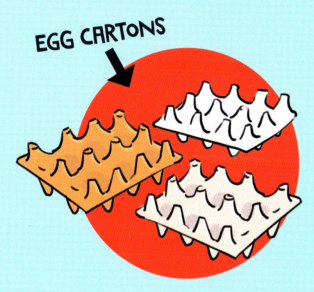

RED PAINT

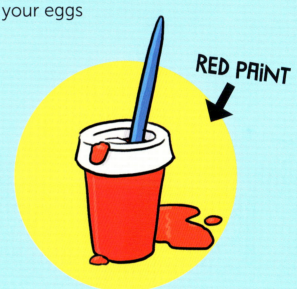

SMALL FIGURINE

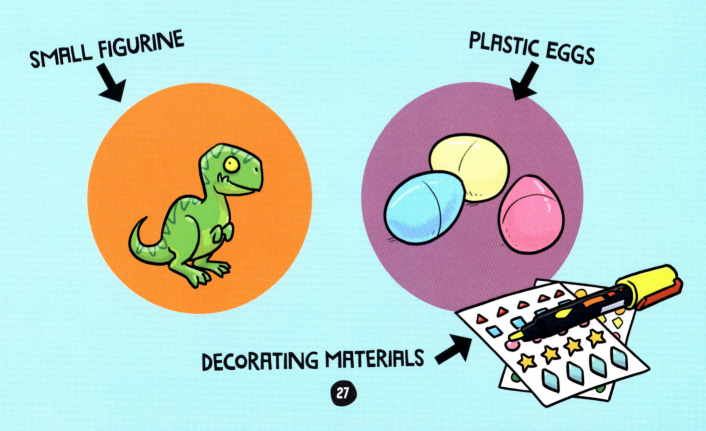

PLASTIC EGGS

DECORATING MATERIALS

GAME
SET UP!

PLACE
THE PLASTIC EGGS
ON THE GRiD.

1

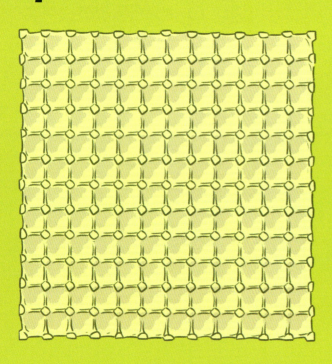

2

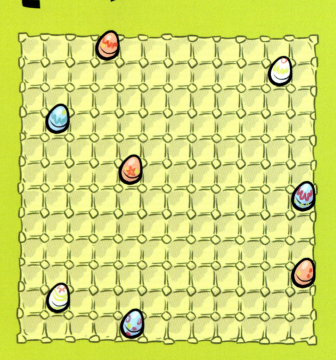

1 Start by taping your egg cartons together into a large grid. The larger the grid, the harder the coding challenge!

2 Place your plastic eggs on the grid. Spread them out. The more plastic eggs you have, the easier your coding challenge will be.

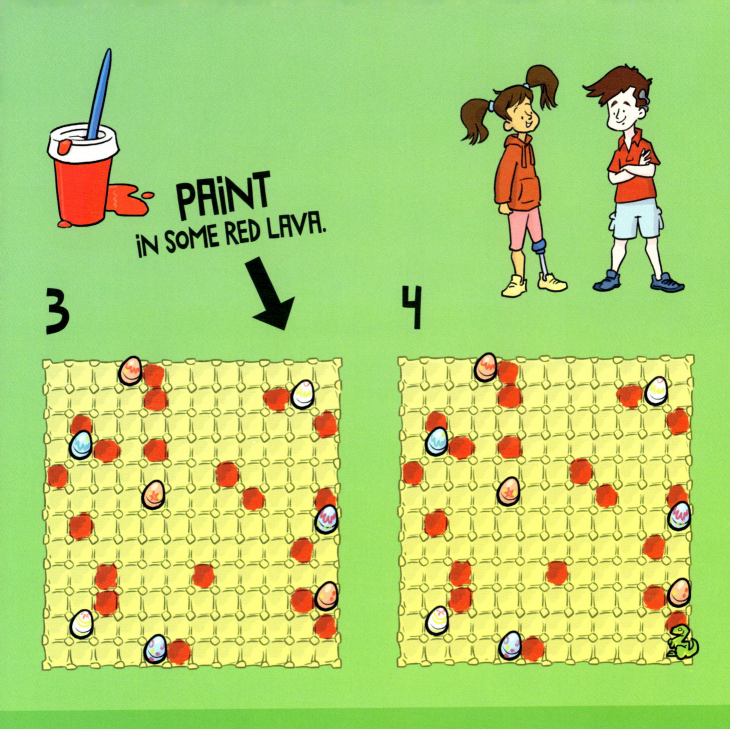

PAINT IN SOME RED LAVA.

3

4

3 Now it's time to paint in some lava. Grab your red paint and paint some of the egg carton grooves red. The more lava you add, the harder the challenge will be. You won't want to put lava on more than a quarter of the available spots.

4 Grab your figurine and start at one corner of your grid.

GAME PLAY: SEQUENCE YOUR ALGORITHM

The **GOAL** of this coding game is to get your figurine to all the prize eggs, while **AVOIDING** the lava spots.

You need to give the instructions to your robot figurine as an '**ALGORITHM**'. You can involve a friend to move the robot around according to your instructions. It's important to give these instructions in the right order (or **SEQUENCE**) so that you don't run into the lava!

AVOID

Once you've reached each prize egg spot, you open it and reveal the prize!

Share the prizes if you're working with friends, or take turns to be the '**CODER**' and the '**MOVER**'.

Here's an **EXAMPLE** of a sequence for the egg carton challenge.

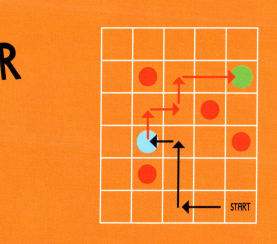

TO GET TO THE BLUE EGG:

* Move left two spaces
* THEN move up two spaces
* THEN move left one space.

TO GET TO THE GREEN EGG FROM THE BLUE EGG:

* Move up one space
* THEN move right one space
* THEN move up one space
* THEN move right two spaces.

← MOVER

CODER

GAME PLAY: EXTRA CHALLENGE!

How about an **EXTRA CHALLENGE**? To make this activity more challenging you'll need to code the entire algorithm in advance. You'll need a piece of paper for this challenge.

Start by writing out all of the instructions needed to get your figure from the start of the grid to every egg on the grid. You won't be able to move the figurine and test out your algorithm until you've written out the whole plan.

Now it's time to test your algorithm! Have a partner move your figurine in the path you outlined on your algorithm. Did you make it through or did you fall in some lava?

TEST YOUR ALGORITHM! ➡

If your algorithm has a mistake, no worries! That's where debugging comes in.

Go back to find the bug in your algorithm so that your sequence works.

DEBUGGING?
GO BACK AND FIND
THAT BUG!

DECOMPOSE THIS!

Decompose this image of a flower wreath!
How many repeated shapes can you find in the
piece of art? Count the number of each shape
and record your totals.

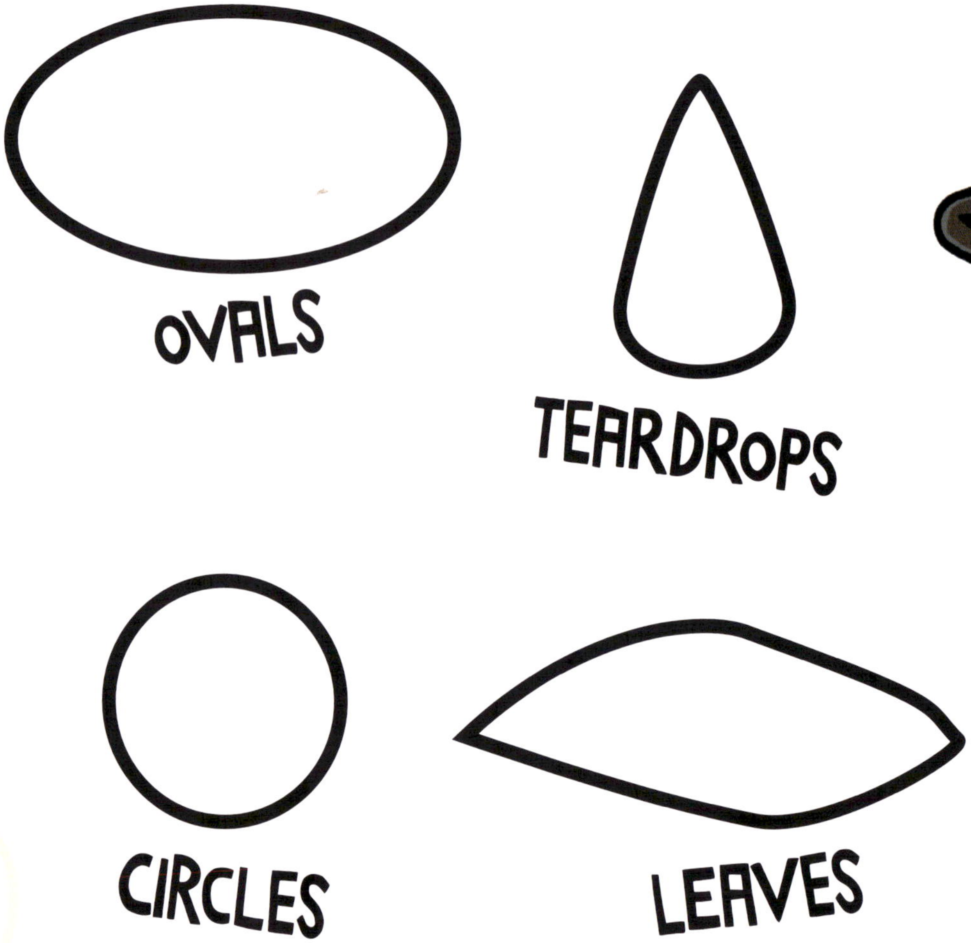

OVALS

TEARDROPS

CIRCLES

LEAVES

(ANSWER ON PAGE 48)

VARIABLES UNPLUGGED!
CODE YOUR OWN PAINTING

In this activity we are going to learn about variables and create beautiful pieces of art at the same time.

Remember that variables are like a box we can hold information in. We are going to use jars to represent our variables and fill them with ideas for **AMAZING ART**.

Once we've sorted our variables, we will create our own unique pieces of art by coding them in an algorithm. Warning! This activity can sometimes lead to **REALLY SILLY RESULTS**.

LET'S GET CREATING!

MATERIALS YOU WILL NEED:

* Blank paper
* 3 to 4 jars
* A pen
* Art materials of your choosing (paints, crayons, pastels)

BLANK PAPER

JARS

PEN

ART MATERIALS

GAME
SET UP!

Start off by labelling your variable jars. In this activity we will use the following variables:

LABEL YOUR JARS.

BACKGROUND SCENERY

ANIMALS

OBJECTS

PEOPLE

Now it's time to fill our variable jars with art ideas. Work as a team to brainstorm at least 10 different ideas you could draw based on the categories on the jars.

For **'BACKGROUND SCENERY'** you might choose:

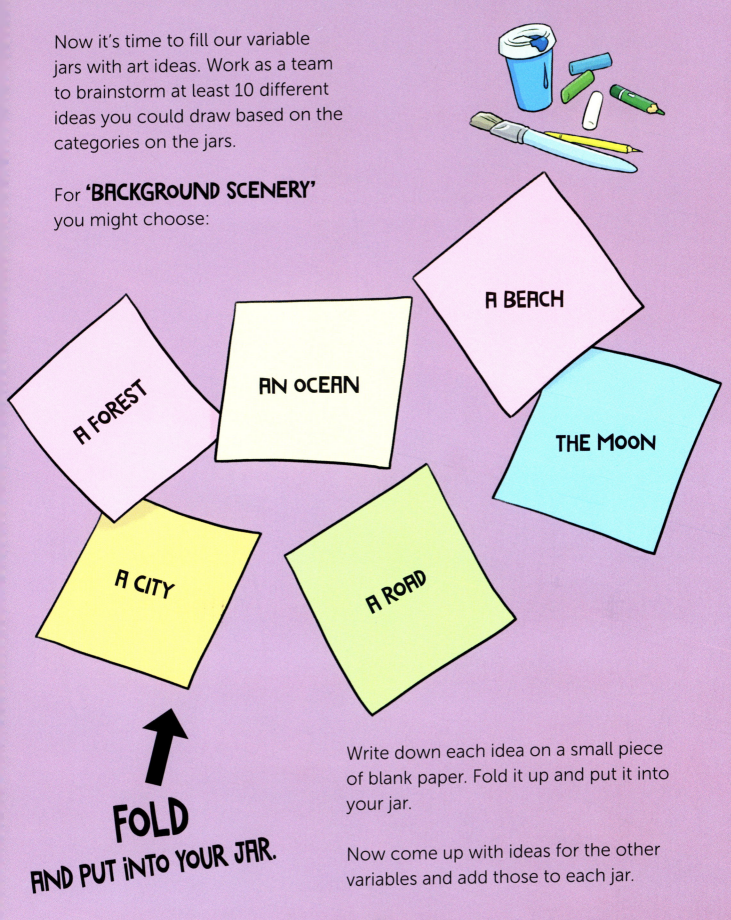

A BEACH

AN OCEAN

A FOREST

THE MOON

A CITY

A ROAD

FOLD
AND PUT INTO YOUR JAR.

Write down each idea on a small piece of blank paper. Fold it up and put it into your jar.

Now come up with ideas for the other variables and add those to each jar.

GAME PLAY:

It's time to code our art algorithm!

Each player picks an art idea from each jar.

Each player must create a piece of art that includes all the ideas you picked out.

BEAR

MOON

GRANDMOTHER

BEACH BALL

TEE HEE HA!

Did your art turn out a bit silly? That's the fun of using random variables! Sometimes we get unexpected results.

SPOT THE BUGS!

This paint-by-numbers is all out of place. Can you help write a true-to-life paint-by-numbers algorithm? Then you can even try to recreate a blank outline of the art yourself on a piece of paper. Give your new algorithm to a friend to see what your debugged algorithm looks like in real life!

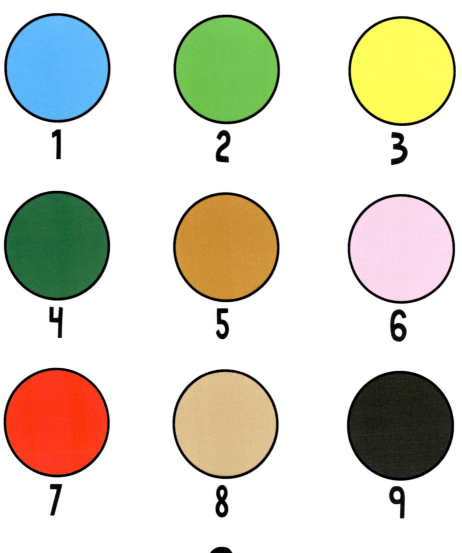

(ANSWER ON PAGE 48)

LET'S **SOLVE** A **CODING PUZZLE!**

We've now learned the basic concepts of coding
and are ready to think just like a computer.

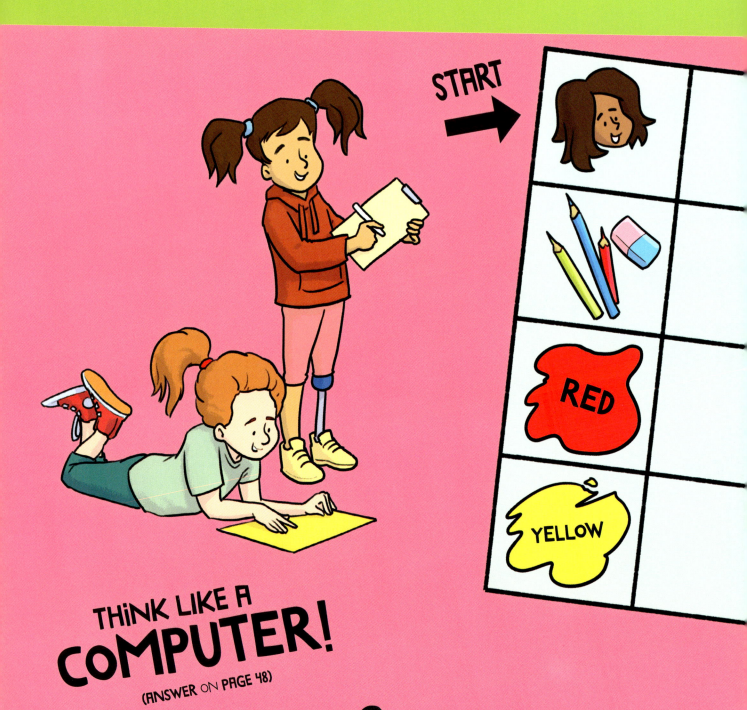

START

THINK LIKE A
COMPUTER!
(ANSWER ON PAGE 48)

In this puzzle, we'll need to use our coding skills to solve a maze and make a rainbow.

Help Lily get to the art studio without running into any obstacles. Along the way, Lily must collect all the colours of the rainbow **iN ORDER**, by coding an algorithm to each colour box.

Write out the algorithm on a separate piece of paper.

COLLECT ALL OF THE COLOURS!

45

GLOSSARY

ALGORITHM:

An algorithm is an instruction given to help complete a certain task.

BRANCHING:

Branching refers to making a decision based on what is happening or has happened.

DEBUG:

Find and solve a problem in coding instructions.

DECOMPOSITION:

Decomposition means breaking down problems into smaller steps.

LOOP:

A set of instructions that repeat until a specific condition is met.

ORIGAMI:

The art of paper folding.

SEQUENCE:

Sequence refers to the order of steps.

VARIABLE:

A variable is a way of holding information. It's like a box that keeps information inside it.

NOTES FOR ADULTS

WHY CODING UNPLUGGED?

Teaching kids to code is a great way to introduce them to the basics of programming and have them learn problem-solving, logic and critical thinking skills. These skills are very applicable in real life, in school, at work or even while they're playing video games!

One of the best ways to begin coding is to learn to code **UNPLUGGED**, so no computer or other hardware is required! By taking coding offline, it's easy to focus on the basic concepts, which are fundamental to learning to code. Combining coding learning with creative or physical activities is a great way to embed the information and keep children active.

FURTHER INFO

FOR MORE FUN CODING BOOKS, WHY NOT TRY ...

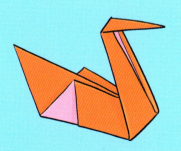

The *Ready, Steady, Code* series (Wayland 2018)

The *Explore AI* series (Wayland, 2021)

AND TRY THIS WEBSITE FOR MORE UNPLUGGED CODING FUN:

www.teachyourkidscode.com

ANSWERS:

PAGE 9:

'Put yellow paint on brush' would be the next step in the sequence.

PAGE 24-25:

Algorithms and sequencing are at work in the cat drawing step-by-step guide.

PAGE 34-35:

Ovals 24
Tear Drops 19
Circles 12
Leaves 37

PAGE 42-43:

1 = dark green
2 = pink
3 = brown
4 = beige
5 = light green
6 = black
7 = blue
8 = yellow
9 = red

PAGE 44-45:

Order of a rainbow is:
RED, ORANGE, YELLOW, GREEN, BLUE, INDIGO, VIOLET

Algorithm:

START ➡ red:
right 1, down 2, left 1

Red ➡ orange:
right 1, up 1, right 1

Orange ➡ yellow:
left 1, down 2, left 1

Yellow ➡ green:
right 2

Green ➡ blue:
right 1, up 2

Blue ➡ indigo:
right 1, up 1

Indigo ➡ violet:
down 1, right 1